MW00629582

# IMAGES
## of America

# WIND CAVE
# NATIONAL PARK
## THE FIRST 100 YEARS

*140*

~~~ *Introductory* ~~~

(*To whomsoever may it read*)

On the first day of January 1891
I saw fit to keep a record of the inside
workings at wind cave, and, acting
with the thought, I started a daily
record which I called (perhaps familiarity)
"The private account of A. J. Mc Donald
permanent guide of Wind Cave".
It was attended to pretty regular until
the busy season "opened up" and then
(through negligence) it was not attended to
but little, and, as a consequence I
will be obliged to describe some of
any exploring trips taken last year
to make a connection with trips made
this year and those of last year that
are recorded. My intention this year is to
keep a correct account of the development and
explorations of wind cave or any other
caverns that fortune favors me to be
exploring in. By the word "exploring"
I mean "finding cavities that no human
-an beings have yet discovered.

Respectfully yours

Z. U. Q.

P. S.

For the meaning of these initials or
any other initials used in the pages
of this book, inquire of the guide
of any of the Celebrated Caverns
of America

The diary of Alvin McDonald was acquired by Wind Cave National Park in 1981 from a family member. The introductory page of that diary shows typical penmanship of the time, as well as a bit of artwork. The meaning of Z.U.Q., Alvin's "secret" code, is not known.

IMAGES
*of America*

# WIND CAVE
# NATIONAL PARK
## THE FIRST 100 YEARS

Peggy Sanders

ARCADIA
PUBLISHING

Copyright © 2003 by Peggy Sanders
ISBN 978-0-7385-2306-4

Published by Arcadia Publishing
Charleston, South Carolina

Printed in the United States of America

Library of Congress Catalog Card Number: 2003101536

For all general information contact Arcadia Publishing at:
Telephone 843-853-2070
Fax 843-853-0044
E-mail sales@arcadiapublishing.com
For customer service and orders:
Toll-Free 1-888-313-2665

Visit us on the Internet at www.arcadiapublishing.com

On January 9, 1903, the Department of the Interior announced the creation of Wind Cave National Park. Before the land achieved national park status, E.A. Hitchcock, Secretary of the Interior, on January 6, 1900, authorized the Commissioner of the General Land Office to withdraw the cave area and approximately 720 acres adjacent to it from public settlement. The initial announcement was for a temporary withdrawal and any bona-fide claimants already on the land were not to be affected.

# CONTENTS

Acknowledgments                                          6

Introduction                                             7

1.    The Early Years                                    9

2.    The Formative Years                               31

3.    Civilian Conservation Corps                       45

4.    Memories and People                               85

5.    Indian Summer Encampments                         91

6.    The Last 50 Years                                103

# ACKNOWLEDGMENTS

Thanks to my husband, Russ, and to our sons and their wives, Carl and Kari Sanders, and Neil and Cris Sanders, for your support. Thank you, Samantha Gleisten at Arcadia Publications, for being such a helpful editor.

The photos used in this publication are mostly from three sources: the archives at Wind Cave National Park, the Suter family, and the Sawyer family. My appreciation goes to Wind Cave staff including Tom Farrell, Chief of Interpretation at Wind Cave; Megan Cherry, Museum Technician Intern; and Mary Laycock. Their assistance and patience were invaluable. Other photos and reference assistance were contributed by the Fall River County Museum, Roy Bledsoe, David Jones, Ray Millard, Ed Renstrom, Dennis Bucher, Bob and Grace Kolterman, David and Cindy Stewart, Barbara Trumball, Russell and Betty Wyatt, Phyllis Scheifer, Yvonne Hollenbeck, Caroline Curl, John Donnell, Dorothy Craft, Diana Nelson, Jim and Marlene Galloway, Mary McDill, and Ruth Ronge. Reference works included *South Dakota History Collections, Volume XXXI*, *Black Hills Engineer Hot Springs Number*, and *South Dakota History, Summer of 2002*.

Estes Suter served as a park ranger, photographer, range manager, and wildlife specialist, among his other duties. Fortunately for us, his photos have been preserved, and enthusiastically offered by his family so that others who love history can benefit from his years of work. John Suter of Hot Springs, South Dakota; Joyce (Suter) Whitcomb from Grand Prairie, Texas; Leonard, Whitmore, California, and their late sister, Bea Voegele, grew up at Wind Cave during the Formative Years and the Civilian Conservation Corps time. Dale Sawyer, the son of park ranger Tom Sawyer, also grew up at the park. He and his wife, Sherrill, invited me to their home in Deerfield, South Dakota (the old Deerfield Store) to share photos and stories. All of their remembrances brought the photos to life.

I am profoundly grateful to the Suter and Sawyer families for their photos as well as oral histories which accompanied the gathering of the photos. It was also very gratifying to reunite John Suter, Dale Sawyer, and Roy Bledsoe (who served with the CCC) after all the years that have passed since they had seen one another. This is another part of history that makes my writing so enjoyable. It is tremendously beneficial that there are people who are anxious to share their personal memories, collections, and mementos in the interest of preserving the past.

# INTRODUCTION

The early discovery of Wind Cave by American Indians brought about several versions of legends concerning the cave. One of the Lakota stories is that buffalo originated in a cave and that Wind Cave was the sacred home of the white buffalo. Another holds that a woman who was a personified buffalo lived in the cave. No matter what is believed, the wind from the cave holds a fascination for all.

Officially, the credit for finding Wind Cave, in the spring of 1881, goes to brothers Jesse and Tom Bingham. John Bohi, historian, gave possible credit to Lame Johnny, who claimed in a leaflet that he found the cave in 1877. However, Anton Snyder, a Wind Cave ranger, wrote in the January 28, 1928 edition of the *Black Hills Engineer* that the Black Hills pioneer John Wells was the one who located the cave. We will follow the official version in this writing.

As the story goes, the Binghams were out deer hunting and Jesse's hat was blown from his head by a gust of wind emitted from an 8-foot-by-10-inch hole in the rock formation. Some days later, Jesse returned to the spot with some friends, and to show off his newly learned trick, he threw his hat up into the air. To his surprise and the amazement of his friends, the hat did not blow into the air, but instead was sucked into the hole. Even with all of the explorations to date, the hat has never been found.

Ownership of the cave became a sore subject in the early years after the discovery. The first location certificates were filed in 1886 by Frank Horton and Nels Hyde who abandoned them soon thereafter. L.C. Faris filed one in 1889. Then a man named Day filed three mining claims on the land in 1890; shortly afterwards, he sold them for the tidy sum of $250 to J.C. Moss, the president of the South Dakota Mining Company. The other partners in the company were M.A. Moss and R.B. Moss, and the same group also owned the Moss Engraving Company in New York City. The claims were dutifully filed and recorded in the office of the Custer County Register of Deeds.

Jesse McDonald and his young adult sons, Elmer and Alvin, were hired by the South Dakota Mining Company to manage the property. It is said that after Moss was called to New York on a family matter, McDonald took over the rights to the property. In 1891, John Stabler and family moved to Hot Springs and there they opened the newly built Parrot Hotel. Once Stabler visited the cave, he thought of the possibilities offered and purchased an interest in the cave.

After the McDonalds' arrival, serious exploration began in the cave and the findings were recorded for us to read. Alvin, variously called Alva or Alvah in some references, kept quite a detailed diary of his ventures into the cave. In January of 1891, he went into the cave 27 times. He became so enamoured with it, that on the days he didn't go in, he felt "homesick" for the cave. Alvin named the rooms, described them in his writings, and exaggerated the distances. To keep from getting lost, he laid down a trail of twine as he went in; he then only had to follow it and gather it up as he went out. Alvin and his companions had to break pieces of rock out of the passages so they could continue their exploits.

The Stablers and the McDonalds feuded intensely for several years over possession of the cave, but the government required that land claimants had to either farm or mine the property. The McDonalds and Stablers did neither, as the land was not right for farming and there were no minerals to mine; thus, the law did not show either family to be bona-fide claimants. The federal government recognized the importance of the site, took possession, and created the first national park focused around a cave.

The cave interior is only one part of the park. The 28,295 acres of prairie and forest are home to an array of plants and animals that are fascinating; put them and the cave together and it's an experience of a lifetime for nature lovers.

Officially, the Great Depression, a severe worldwide economic downturn, began in October of 1929 and ended at the beginning of World War II. However, on the Great Plains it actually began years before due to the fact that a depression in the agricultural sector started in 1923. The crop and commodity prices were very low, farms were foreclosed upon, and banks failed. In the early 1930s, drought of unheard of proportions grasped the Heartland. The winds were horrendous too and dirt blew so badly that the era was dubbed, "The Dirty Thirties."

The Civilian Conservation Corps (CCC) had an immeasurable impact all across the United States. Due to the Great Depression and a devastating long-term drought, people had no jobs, no money, and no food. President Franklin D. Roosevelt created a program called "The New Deal," which included the Civilian Conservation Corps. This program took unemployed and skillless young men and taught them trades so they could go out into the workforce. On July 16, 1934, CCC Camp NP-1, Wind Cave, Company 2754 was established. Within two weeks, 240 men were at the camp, living in tents. The workers soon built their own camp including a mess hall, supply building, bath house and laundry, recreation hall, two latrines, hospital, headquarters building, garage, and eight barracks. These 1937 Ford trucks provided transportation for the "Cs," as they were called, to get to some of their worksites within the park. Only the men who are standing are identified and they are, from left to right, Slim Larson, Roy Bledsoe, Tom Sawyer, and Bob Augustine.

# One

# THE EARLY YEARS

This is the hole in the rock that started it all. Strong currents of air caused by changes in atmospheric pressure rush in and out of the cave. A falling barometer usually causes the wind to blow out of the entrance, and a rising barometer causes it to blow in. The cave is outlined in Pahasapa limestone; over thousands of years, cracks and seams in the limestone were gradually enlarged by water. The cave extends down to table and except for some slight seepage the cave is mostly dry. Wind Cave was the first park established by the federal government to protect a cave.

Tom Bingham is generally credited with the discovery of the cave early in the spring of 1881. On the day the cave was found, Tom's brother, Jesse, and their half-brother, John Dennis, were along on the excursion. Whether Tom or Jesse actually made the discovery is not truly known; Jesse had a less than stellar reputation due to charges of stealing cattle, so the credit may have been passed on to Tom.

Jesse McDonald's family was a hard luck outfit from Franklin County, Iowa, where Elmer and Alvin were born. In 1888, Jesse, pictured here, went to Thermopolis, Wyoming with these two young men to find work. They left the rest of the family, the mother, sister, and three other brothers, in Calliope, Iowa. By the fall of 1889, the three men moved to Four Mile, also called Moss City, near present day Custer, South Dakota. R.B. Moss was the man of the town and he hired the McDonalds to work at Wind Cave on behalf of the South Dakota Mining Company.

At the age of 17 years, Alvin McDonald was the first serious explorer to record his explorations. Unfortunately he died in 1893 at only 20 years old from a case of typhoid fever complicated by pneumonia. His obituary in the *Custer County Chronicle* called him, "the chief guide at Wind Cave, always courteous and accommodating."

Alvin McDonald was laid to rest on a bluff that overlooks the entrance to the cave. A statue of the young man was carved in sandstone by Mr. Reardon of Buffalo Gap and placed at the gravesite. In later years, the statue was removed by officials because it had been damaged.

The Tally-ho Coach was actually a brand name of the coach. C.L. (Chris) Jensen of Hot Springs owned an early tourism venture, stage lines to Cascade and to Wind Cave. An advertisement listing the services stated: "Arrangements for Guides, Lights, etc. may be made at the Jensen Livery and Stage Company Office, Opposite the Evans Hotel. Daily Coaches are run to the Cave, leaving at 8:30 am. Phone No. 6. " October 17, 1895, was the date of the articles of incorporation for the People's Telephone and Telegraph Company, owned by Chris Jensen. The company was so successful that it stood on its own until a merger with Golden West Companies was completed January 2, 1982.

As stage passengers and other visitors approached the Wind Cave buildings, this is the view they encountered. If Jensen, a renowned storyteller, was aboard, he regaled the passengers with his imaginative stories.

Jensen ran a thriving business with several coaches making the run to Wind Cave. He also ran coaches to Cascade, a hopeful and bustling town south of Hot Springs. The Petty Brothers had coaches that originated at the Burlington and Elkhorn railroad depot in Buffalo Gap. Their routes also went to Wind Cave, Hot Springs, and Cascade.

13

Chris Jensen is at the reins of the coach. John Stablers is on the right.

The 16-by-18-foot log house at the foot of the stairs was built by the McDonalds. The entrance to the cave was covered by a trap door. Depending on the air movement within the cave, at times it was nearly impossible to open that door.

William Jennings Bryan and the governor of Nebraska were on one of the early tours. Bryan was a politician from Nebraska. Records show he was in the Hot Springs area at least twice, the first time in 1892 when this photo was taken. He is later mentioned as visiting Hot Springs on October 14, 1914, while he was the U.S. Secretary of State. Bryan is in the front with a child sitting on his lap. John Stabler is on the far right. Katie Stabler is seated behind John. The governor is between the two men.

This photo was taken in the Post Office Room, so named because of the small cubby-hole-like boxes that adorn the room. Early tours, at a cost of $2 per person, were taken by candlelight; candles were carried by each person in the touring group. This photo erroneously notes, "1 mile from the entrance, 400 feet from surface."

Ethlyn and Della Stabler, daughters of George and Minnie Stabler, grew up near the cave and spent hours exploring above and below the ground.

STEVENS
PHOTS.

METHODIST CHURCH
WIND CAVE, S.D.

Rooms inside the cave were named by guides as well as by visitors. Naming the rooms simplified record-keeping, tour plans, and discussions. The Methodist Church Room was where the first religious services were held inside the cave. The formation shown is called boxwork.

The old entrance building was at the foot of the walkway. The headgear was worn by visitors to protect their heads from the low hanging rocks as they ventured through the cave and to keep the dust out of their hair. In this 1917 photo, the woman in the front left, wearing the dark dress appears to be Grace (Tillotson) Stewart, great aunt of the author. Family lore tells that years earlier, Grace was the first child to enter Wind Cave. Typical of oral history, this story cannot be proven, but there is written information that her family visited the cave very early on, with the McDonalds.

17

The Wind Cave Hotel was a one-and-a-half-story building with rough lumber on the outside. It measured 22-by-32 feet. The hotel was originally run by the Stabler family, who abandoned the business in October of 1903. In 1909, the hotel was refurbished, with construction of a new roof on the west wing, replacement of several windows, and whitewashing of the exterior.

A new entrance building was constructed to replace the McDonald building. The wooden walkway continued to ease the path to the entrance.

To create a water system leading to the headquarters reservoir, four feet of muck had to be removed from the spring. Without the water system, any water necessary had to be hauled 2.5 miles.

Teams of horses were used to remove the muck to improve the spring for the water system.

On June 29, 1903, South Dakota Congressman Eben W. Martin recommended that William A. Rankin be named the first superintendent of Wind Cave National Park. The Secretary of the Interior concurred and Rankin assumed the job on August 1, 1903. Out of the entire park's appropriation of $2500, Rankin's salary was $75. He remained in the job for nearly 6 years. Mrs. Rankin was allowed to use the hotel for a concession area. Her lunches cost 50¢. The concession contracts continued through 1908 and the hotel was torn down in 1913.

Ribbon stalactites, also called cave bacon, hang from the ceiling, reminiscent of icicles. They form ribbons because they grow on slanting ceilings, instead of more level horizontal ceilings. Stalagmites (not shown) grow up from the floor of the cave.

Joseph E. Pilcher became the second superintendent of Wind Cave, taking over from William Rankin. Pilcher resided on a ranch west of Custer, where he patented a mining claim. His son, Rufus, succeeded him as superintendent on April 26, 1910, after Joseph suddenly died on March 14 of that year.

The Pilcher family carried their candles as they toured the cave, stopping in the IOOF or Odd Fellows Hall. The room was initially reported to be 170–175 feet below the surface, although it is known now the true depth at that point is 208 feet. Mother Jan Pilcher, in the center right of the photo, had on black gloves. Warren Pilcher is the second from the right in the rear, and Pete Paulsen is in the right front. Paulsen was a guide.

| WIND CAVE | CITY LIVERY |
|---|---|

GARAGE 'PHONE No 142.

# PERCY WILKINS

## HOT SPRINGS
## SO. DAK.

Auto Stand 'Phone No. 100--Three Rings
At Evans Hotel Corner.

47188944

This business card was donated to the Wind Cave archives by local contractor Ken Pourier. He found it in a wall cavity behind old plaster while he was doing some renovation work in an area building.

## DRIVES.

—

### Wind Cave.
Twenty-four Mile Trip
Hours for entering Cave are
9 a. m. and 2 p. m. daily.
Fare, round trip $2.50 each

—

### Fall River Falls.
Ten mile trip.    The finest scenery
near Hot Springs

—

### Cascade Springs
Twenty-two Mile Trip

—

### Cheyenne River Falls
Thirty Mile Trip

—

Points of Interest in Hot Springs.
National Sanitarium
State Soldiers' Home
Two Large Plunges
Residence District
The Siloam Baths

821.

The reverse side of the Percy Wilkins business card details the facts of early tourism in the Hot Springs area. The Cheyenne River Falls was later covered by the waters of Angostura Dam, when it was constructed in the 1940s–early 1950s.

Between October 1, 1921 and September 30, 1922, visitation totaled 21,016. Transportation had improved to include small buses such as the one pictured here. Camping numbers also increased.

As time went on, visitors to the park often drove their own vehicles. After the white rocks on the hill were arranged, Wind Cave staff sent a photo like this to the Department of Interior. DOI soon wrote and told the staff to remove the rock sign as it was not "natural" looking. Among the visitors during this era was J.A. (John) Stanley, a newspaper man from Lead, South Dakota. Stanley later moved to Hot Springs where he published the *Hot Springs Star*. In the same entourage were U.S. Senator Peter Norbeck, Col. Shade from the South Dakota Highway Commission, and Dr. C.C. O'Hara, then-president of the South Dakota School of Mines in Rapid City.

The information booths were helpful for the many visitors who came to the park without tour guides. The first car is a 1927 or 1928 Chevrolet and the one behind it is a Model A Ford.

Esther Brazell, the wife of Thomas, became a park ranger at Wind Cave. She served in 1914 and 1919. She may have been the first woman ranger in the entire park service. Thomas Brazell was the superintendent for 19 months, beginning August 1, 1914.

A more practical method of lighting the paths during tours was the use of lanterns instead of candles. The candles tended to blow out and the lanterns had glass globes that prevented blowouts.

Another early lighting method consisted of drilling a candle-sized hole in metal pails and sticking a candle up through the hole. The bucket protected the candle's flame. The fashions of the day did not seem to allow for casual clothing, even on tours of the cave.

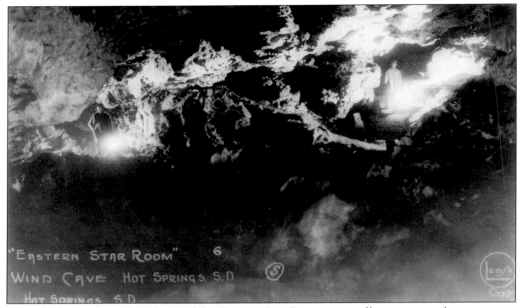

"EASTERN STAR ROOM" 6
WIND CAVE HOT SPRINGS, S.D
HOT SPRINGS S.D

If you look closely at this photo of the Eastern Star Room, you will see men in the cave areas that seem to be lit up. Some rooms in the cave were named after organizations.

A great portion of the photos of the interior of Wind Cave were taken in this room, the Odd Fellows Hall, because it is such a spacious area, conducive to accommodating good sized groups. It is located one-quarter-mile inside the length of the cave. The man in the bottom left of the photo may have been a freed Civil War slave who came north.

October of 1925 brought O.F. Hill, a representative for the Neutrowound Radio Manufacturing Company, and A.C. Williams, who was a salesman from the Sioux Falls Dakota Iron Store, to Wind Cave. Their purpose was to take a radio down into the cave and find out if it would receive stations. The initial challenge was the fact that there was no place to attach a "ground," which was necessary to make the radio work. Further, the iron in the cave walls and the air cells of the honeycomb caused even more difficulties. In the end, KOA of Denver came in loud and clear. The Dallas, Texas, station, WRR, was the most distant station picked up. Hill and Williams, and Superintendent and Mrs. Brazell, along with rangers Snyder and McCain and others, were on the excursion. This photo is the cover of the book.

The Odd Fellows Hall was one of the early rooms named after local organizations. It was also called the Model Room. The name came from a resemblance to one of the lodge's emblems.

A band from Winner, South Dakota, took their instruments into the cave in 1926 and performed a few numbers in the Model Room.

The room known as Swiss Scenery is 50-feet long and 15-feet tall. The boxwork is rather rough compared to the surrounding rooms and is it shaded from yellow to dark brown.

The Elks Lodge Room is more accurately known as the Elk's Room, also called Elk's Resort, and Scenes of Widow. The name comes from the formation that resembles an elk's head.

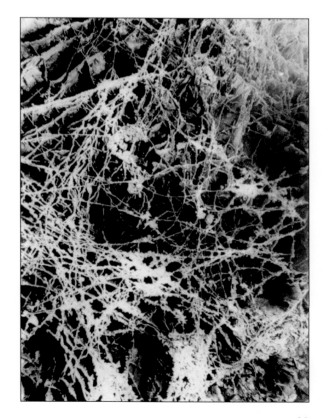

The ceiling of the Elk's Room features intricate boxwork.

On August 10, 1912, Congress passed the National Game Preserve Act, thereby establishing a National Game Preserve at Wind Cave National Park. At the same time, the American Bison Society agreed to present the park with a herd of 14 bison, which were delivered from the New York Zoological Society in 1913. The following year, 21 head of elk were transplanted from Jackson Hole, Wyoming, and the Boone and Crocket Club of New York sent antelope. This house was the residence of a park ranger and his family, in this case, Estes Suter. The Game Preserve was disbanded on July 1, 1935 and that land was transferred to Wind Cave National Park. After the preserve ceased to exist the house was moved to Hot Springs and placed at its present location, 538 Lincoln.

Jim Lynam, left, and Barney Curl were employees of the U.S. Biological Survey, which ran the Game Preserve or Game Ranch as it was known. Barney worked there from 1929 to 1935. After he and Caroline Albright were married on April 1, 1934, they lived at Wind Cave for a year.

## Two

# THE FORMATIVE YEARS

The Beaver Creek Bridge is located on South Dakota Highway 87, just 2 miles north of the Wind Cave Visitor Center. The spandrel concrete arch was built in 1929. It is 225 feet long and sits 115 feet from the floor of Beaver Creek Canyon.

The bridge was designed by J.E. Kirkham, the South Dakota bridge engineer at the time. Even though U.S. Senator Peter Norbeck was no longer in state government, he retained a good deal of influence on projects that were dear to him. The placement of the bridge was one of those projects. This is the only bridge of its type in South Dakota, thus it is historically significant.

The senator insisted that the highway be turned to the south along the river in the canyon in order to achieve a spectacular view of the bridge, visible for at least one quarter of a mile away. Constructing the bridge in this manner cost more than the standard crossing—a triple-ten-by-ten box culvert installed at the head of the canyon—would have cost.

The brakes failed!

Fortunately, the pickup high-centered and stopped before it went over the cliff. The unknown gentleman was able to open his door and step out—gingerly.

Undoubtedly the undercarriage was severely damaged and a wrecker was necessary to extricate the pickup.

Lake Ta-Tan-Ka was the result of an earthen dam built on Cold Spring Creek in the northern area of the park by the U.S. Biological Survey, an agency of the Department of Agriculture. Senator Norbeck backed the construction and it was named Norbeck Dam. However, the dam was constructed over a porous rock area and it did not hold water well at all. It was nicknamed, "Peter's Puddle," which is how locals always referred to the water hole. It was breached in 1989.

Tom Sawyer, on the left, and an unidentified man were on horseback in front of the ranger's dorm. A 1930 Chevrolet pickup sits off to the side.

Tom Sawyer, his aunt, and her friend are pictured standing beside an Essex-6 car. These American Motors Corporation cars were built from 1919 to 1932. The photo was taken in 1929 or 1930.

A natural spring supplied water to an underground concrete tank reservoir that is still in use. Workers installed a pipeline water main by hand. The gravity flow from the reservoir above the buildings provided excellent pressure right to the houses. However, it was not piped into the homes, but to hydrants just outside. Chemical toilets were used inside the homes.

A newer administration building, including a concession area, is shown along with the superintendent's house across the road.

Dale Sawyer, in the National Guard uniform, stands next to a 1935 Ford with his dad, Tom Sawyer, in his ranger uniform.

Ranger Tom Sawyer took a breather after fighting a fire in the park.

Estes Suter was a park ranger with the National Park Services, serving at various locations throughout his career. From February 1, 1931 to October 1944, he served his first stint at Wind Cave. After Mount Rushmore came under the jurisdiction of the Department of the Interior in November of 1944, Ranger Suter was transferred there. From July 27, 1948 through January 7, 1953, he was the first superintendent at the Badlands National Monument. When he returned to Wind Cave on January 8, 1953, until his retirement November 23, 1963, he was the chief ranger.

As one of his many duties, Estes Suter was put in charge of managing and improving the park's buffalo herd during his first tenure. He knew that when the buffalo roamed the plains, nature used selective breeding and that is what he set out to do. This buffalo bull was the product of several years of selective breeding.

Watching the herds was one of Estes' most valuable management tools. He spent hours observing their mannerisms, patterns, habits, and body confirmation. These learning sessions helped immensely as he watched for strengths and weaknesses, choosing which animals he would use for breeding stock and which ones he would remove from the herd.

A park ranger would not handle a healthy baby bison, but this one was crippled. Its front feet turned under and it had to be assisted by putting temporary splints on the legs that helped strengthen and train the feet. Estes believed this was a flaw in the breeding so, in an attempt to weed out the weak genes, he did not re-breed the cow.

These men were preparing for the annual bison roundup in 1936. From left, the men seated on the vehicle fenders are Estes Suter, wildlife and range manager; Everett (Ep) Howe, CCC; Edward Freeland, park superintendent; unidentified CCC man; John Chambers; and an unidentified CCC man. The two men in the rear at the far left are also unidentified CCC men.

These crates on the truck were the method by which bison, elk, antelope, and other wildlife was transported to the Game Preserve at Wind Cave National Park.

In 1936, vehicles driven by Estes Suter, Tom Sawyer, and Superintendent Freeland, rounded up the buffalo for their herd health work, such as testing for diseases.

The buffalo corrals were solidly built and designed for safety of both the men and the buffalo.

Because bison are wild and dangerous animals—unpredictable, fast, and powerful—the men did not get down into the pens with the animals. Instead they worked from catwalks.

The tail on the buffalo signals he is mad, probably because he doesn't appreciate being confined. It was a wise and cautious man who herded the animal from the catwalk.

Estes Suter was enamored with all aspects of wildlife. If he needed to get a better look at something to increase his knowledge or to check for problems, he always found a way to achieve his goal.

Something deserved a closer look so Estes threw a rope up, caught it securely on a rock, and pulled himself up. After he was on the cliff he was able to get a good look at the object of his wildlife search, a falcon nest.

Not only was the animal wildlife important to Estes, and part of his job, so was the grasslands that supported that wildlife. He collected and pressed for preservation a sample of every plant within the park. His collection ultimately went to the University of Wyoming.

The prairie and the park is pictured here as seen and treasured by Estes Suter, Tom Sawyer, and all of their fellow rangers throughout the years. Currently, about 90,000 people visit the cave annually and many more drive the park roads.

*Three*

# CIVILIAN
# CONSERVATION CORPS

The Civilian Conservation Corps had few mechanized tools—shovels and other hand tools were mostly what they used. The government had two basic goals when the CCC, and other work forces, were established. The men needed jobs and training, and many natural resources needed attention. By 1932, 25 percent of American men between the ages of 15 to 24 had only part-time jobs, because there were no full-time jobs available. In South Dakota alone, a total of 31,097 people, including enrollees, veterans, and supervisory and office personnel, had been employed between April 1933 and July of 1942, when the CCC was disbanded.

CCC enrollees were mostly unmarried young men. The allowed age range from 1933 to 1935 was 18 to 25 years old. During the years 1935 to 1937, accepted ages were 17 to 28, and the last change was to 17 years old to 25, put in place July 1, 1937. World War I veterans made up a good number of the veterans' section. Veterans were not restricted to being single. A third category was called Local Experienced Men (LEMs). These men worked with the general enrollees and veterans as they learned new trades.

They all knew the business end of a shovel. Enrollees were paid $30 per month, were housed, clothed, fed, and had their medical needs met. Because they were working to also gain money to support their families, enrollees were required to send $25 home to help their parents in the time of the horrendous economic depression. Veterans and LEMs were paid their full amounts each month.

Conditions were not always easy, but the men at least had food and shelter and could help provide the same for their loved ones. This work detail was assigned to a forestry area to remove brush, jack pines, and excess trees, work which ultimately created magnificent stands of timber. In South Dakota alone more than 200,000 acres of pine trees were worked in this manner.

It was not all work and no play. These CCC men were swimming in the Norbeck Dam—locally known as, "Peter's Puddle"—inside the park. Enrollees were not supposed to bring cars to camps, but many tales have been told of cars being parked and covered with tree branches only to mysteriously disappear on weekends. The men were not always assigned to camps near their homes. Camps were administered by the U.S. Army, with one or more officers in charge. However, the priority was given to the work at hand. Army-related aspects involved organization only, and they included reveille at 6 a.m. and meals served by the clock, but there was little else military-related in the camps. On Saturday nights, men from the camp would pile into Army trucks and ride into Hot Springs to attend dances. The men would get all cleaned up, but by the time they had ridden in the back of a truck on the dirt road, they were usually plenty dusty upon arrival.

When most of the camps first opened, men slept in tents while they built needed buildings. This was one of several barracks at Wind Cave. Carpentry was one of the first skills taught—by local contractors hired to do the actual construction since the enrollees did not have the skills. Building supplies were purchased locally, giving a boost to the area's economy. After the 8-hour work days were completed, the men had access to boxing equipment, cards, volleyball, and various activities. Their daily jobs kept them in top physical condition. Several camps had baseball teams and the competition between camps was intense.

Barracks' interiors looked pretty much the same from camp to camp once the buildings were constructed. Army orderliness was observed, as visible in the placement of the boots under the bunk. Although the furnishings were sparse, they were sufficient, dry and out of the wind. The big wood stove helped, though the exteriors were only one-inch sheeting, often covered with tar paper or creosote. Some were painted brown or green. The wooden barracks housed between 25 and 50 men.

The CCC camp was located northeast of the visitor center in the photo. This visitor center and the elevator building were built at a later time than is indicated in this sequence of photos, but they are shown here to give a point of reference to the reader. The largest house was the superintendent's home. The smallest building was the diesel power house, which contained a four-cylinder diesel engine. The engine could move the elevator, but when that was in use it couldn't do much else. When a ranger wanted to utilize the elevator, he had to call ahead to "reserve" the power from the engine.

Between early August 1934 and October 6 of that same year, CCC 2753, the camp at Wind Cave, was constructed, consisting of: 8 barracks, each 20 by 60 feet; 2 latrines measuring 12 by 20 feet; and a T-shaped building with a 20-by-60-foot mess or dining hall and a 20-by-80-foot kitchen and storeroom. Other buildings constructed during the same time frame included a supply building with cooks' quarters, a bath house and laundry, an infirmary, a headquarters building, technical service quarters, a garage, and a recreation hall. This made for quite a concentration of buildings in that one little spot.

# Certificate of Discharge

## from

## Civilian Conservation Corps

TO ALL WHOM IT MAY CONCERN:

THIS IS TO CERTIFY THAT * ROY N. BLEDSOE   CC 7-244,318 , A MEMBER OF THE

CIVILIAN CONSERVATION CORPS, WHO WAS ENROLLED April 19th, 1937 AT
(Date)

Co.2754,CCC,NP-1,Hot Springs, S. Dak, IS HEREBY DISCHARGED THEREFROM, BY REASON

OF ** Honorably - Expiration of term of enrollment, having served over eighteen months.

SAID ROY N. BLEDSOE WAS BORN IN Oral ,

IN THE STATE OF South Dakota WHEN ENROLLED HE WAS 17 11/12 YEARS

OF AGE AND BY OCCUPATION A Farm Laborer HE HAD Blue EYES,

Light HAIR, Ruddy COMPLEXION, AND WAS Five FEET

Eight INCHES IN HEIGHT. HIS COLOR WAS White

GIVEN UNDER MY HAND AT Co. 2754, CCC, NP-1 , THIS Thirty-first DAY
Hot Springs, S. Dak.

OF March , ONE THOUSAND NINE HUNDRED AND Thirty-nine

_Gordon I. Henry_ - Commanding Officer
(Name)                    (Title)

C.C.C. Form No. 2
April 5, 1933

GORDON I. HENRY, 1st Lieut.  Inf-Res. 7th CA

*Insert name, as "John J. Doe".
**Give reason for discharge.        3—10171

# RECORD OF SERVICE IN CIVILIAN CONSERVATION CORPS

**Served:

a. From  4/19/37  to  3/31/39 , under  Interior  Dept. at Co. 2754, CCC, NP-1
Hot Springs, S. Dak.

Type of work  Truck driving  * Manner of performance  Excellent

b. From  to , under  Dept. at

Type of work  * Manner of performance

c. From  to  under  Dept. at

Type of work  * Manner of performance

d. From  to  under  Dept. at

Type of work  * Manner of performance

e. From  to  under  Dept. at

Type of work  * Manner of performance

Remarks:  Absence with leave: 12/29/38 to 1/2/39 incl. and 1/23/39 to 1/28/39 incl.
Absence without leave: None.  Absence without pay: None.
Rating - Member  Address of enrollee: Oral, S. Dak.
Due U. S. M/R..$0.12  Due Company Fund.....$4.00

The Project Superintendent, Mr. Roy Sackett makes the following estimate
of enrollee Bledsoe as a workman: Excellent.  Address of Mr. Sackett;
Hot Springs, S. Dak.

INELIGIBLE FOR RESELECTION HAVING SERVED OVER EIGHTEEN MONTHS.

Discharged:  March 31, 1939  at Co. 2754, CCC, NP-1, Hot Springs, S. Dak.

Transportation furnished from  None desired.  to
Fort Snelling. Minn.

APR 13 1939

Paid in full  0.88  Gordon I Henry  Comdg. C.2754

*Use words "Excellent", "Satisfactory", or "Unsatisfactory".  GORDON I. HENRY, 1st Lieut. Inf-Res. 7th CASC.
**To be taken from C. C. C. Form No. 1.  (Name)  (Title)

W. A. ENOS. CAPT.  F.D.
Finance Officer.  U.S. GOVERNMENT PRINTING OFFICE  3—10171

Assistant

The camp is seen here in relation to the elevator building. Note the lack of trees in this 1934 photo. According to an oral history given by Charles Moode, who worked on the elevator shaft during the winter of 1934–35, he helped tie reinforcing steel and move sand to mix the concrete.

The elevator building was one of the buildings constructed by the CCC, at a total cost of $18,086.62. It consists of lobby, first aid room, comfort stations, transformer room, and a heater room on the main floor. The motor generator room was on the second floor, with the elevator equipment on the top, also called the penthouse floor. Except for the frame door, the building is fireproof.

Work began on the elevator shaft in 1934. Some references say there was no dynamite used. Either way it was dug by men with shovels, and the dirt was removed one bucketful at a time, to the depth of 204 feet. But Charles Moode and others said dynamite was used in making the elevator shaft. Moode said, "I was a powder monkey for the blasting. Holes were drilled 12 to 18 inches into the rock and half sticks of powder were inserted. The charges were kept weak because we only wanted to crack the rock. Then the rock was removed by hand. The shaft was covered with a wooden platform that was recessed into the pit. A small trap door, about 3-feet square, was constructed in the center of the platform. The men entered the shaft by riding on a 50-gallon steel barrel attached to a cable and winch. It must have been quite a ride! The barrel would swing back and forth, and the men would quickly have to push themselves off the sides of the shaft as they ascended or descended. An alternative method of getting up and down within the shaft was to climb on the form work or the reinforcing."

This hoist or head rig, as it was called, was stationary over the hole as it was being dug down into the Garden of Eden level in the cave. As the hole got deeper the wooden frame was replaced with a steel one. Temporary shaft timbers were installed then replaced with a concrete shaft lining. The addition of the elevator allowed tours to make a one-way trip through the cave instead of having to double back.

The men poured footings and made building forms for the retaining wall in the early stages of building. There were no accidents that caused lost time during the 10-month construction period of the elevator building.

Since the building was started on March 1, the aggregate and water were both heated to keep them from freezing so work could continue. The construction took 210 working days or 4,900 man-days at $2 per day.

Once the foundations were completed, the stone work began with a crew of 10 men cutting and 6 men laying the stone. The stone mason foreman was Scott Hill and the men he trained were able to go out into the workforce as experienced stone cutters after their CCC training was completed, fulfilling one of the purposes of the CCC. This photo was taken March 15, 1934.

As the building progressed upwards the temporary tin structure was removed. Note the steel "I" beams in the penthouse portion of the building. Tile was placed around the shaft and on the inside of the stone walls during cold weather.

One-foot square adzed timbers were put in place to support the porch roof. An adze is a hand tool, somewhat resembling an ax, and it is usually used to smooth rough lumber. The adzeman swings the tool between his legs and strikes the timbers.

George Miller from Minnekata was one of the adzemen on the Wind Cave projects, including the timbers inside the visitor center which was also built during the CCC years. He learned the trade on a railroad bridge gang. George later went on to become the mayor of Hot Springs.

The first pair of rafters was put in place in order to make the proper alignment for the flashing between the stone wall and the wood roof.

A corner of the open sided area, or loggia, shows the type of stonework pattern used in the elevator building. The sandstone was locally quarried.

When the front portion of the building was nearly completed, the landscaping began with grading of the soil, sodding of grass, and planting of shrubs.

Work was suspended at this point in the construction due to the visitors during tourist season, which officially began on May 24.

On September 15, 1934, after the heavy travel season was over, work resumed on the back side of the building. The men worked as diligently and quickly as possible, with the knowledge that winter and severe weather were not too far away.

The remaining temporary metal structure was removed, the Otis elevator hoist was set in, and the stonework got as far as the penthouse floor in October of 1934.

A park trail led to the front portion of the elevator building. The tiles that can be seen on the building later had a stucco finish applied.

A reinforced concrete slab was poured over the penthouse. To move the concrete, a runway walk was built from the hilltop south of the building.

When the temporary penthouse structure was removed, the hoisting equipment was tightly enclosed to keep out dirt and moisture in order to keep the equipment in good operating condition.

The completed penthouse, the hoist, and the switch boards are shown. This section of the building is heated by an air duct coming from the furnace room on the main floor.

The selector for the Otis elevator is shown in the right side of the photo. Even though the elevator was installed in 1935, it took until 1938 to totally finish the building.

The control panel and relay stations for the Otis elevator were cumbersome. The controls were placed in dust proof cabinets.

This is the view through the loggia toward the terrace. Dirt areas were planted with wild spirea to control erosion and to naturally beautify the area.

The corner stone was set during a dedication ceremony in the spring of 1938. A recessed area in the top of the stone houses a time capsule with the history of the building and elevator construction.

This photo shows the lobby looking toward the west exit and the first aid room. The comfort station door is shown on the left wall.

This is the view from the lobby while looking through the arch into the hall and the elevator area.

The west end of the building has a covered seating area which provides a lovely view and resting stop.

The completed elevator building including landscaping is shown here.

This is the walk-in entrance. The natural entrance is only 14 inches-by-20 inches—not large enough for anyone to enter. The McDonalds pierced into the earth and created this opening, near the natural entrance. The new entrance was covered by a trap door.

This "natural looking" entrance door was put in during 1936, replacing the trap door and old wooden building. When the door is open, it looks like an inviting entrance.

In the closed position, the bars on the door add to the security of the cave.

Kimball's Music Hall contains a great amount of boxwork; some of the boxes are closed and look like honeycomb. The room has also been called McKinley Memorial Hall, with the Wind Cave Chimes. In his diary, Alvin McDonald wrote of the "Chamber of Bells," and from the description of his route, it appears that he was referring to this room, possibly meaning that the boxwork reminded him of bells.

Copyright, 1935, A. & N. Literary Club., Wash., D. C.

Hot Springs, S. D.

NAME ...*Ray Millard*...

SERIAL NO. ...*7-150-237*...

RATING ...*Public Contact Man*...

DETAIL NO. ...*Park Serv Hdqtrs*...

Ray Millard served with the CCC at Wind Cave in 1935. This was his identification card, which shows his title, but he said his job was "tour guide and latrine sergeant." He later sent a large group of photos taken in the camp to Wind Cave where they are now archived. In addition, he mailed a long, descriptive letter that told the details of each photo. The donation has been a tremendous help in detailing the history of the Civilian Conservation Corps.

The wooden walkways to the cave entrance were replaced by this limestone bridge constructed by the CCC. This side view shows why a bridge was necessary.

Viewing the bridge construction from this angle shows the supports, the stonework pattern, and the hand tools that were such a necessary part of the CCC work.

The foot bridge on the trail from the administration building to the cave entrance was completed in June of 1936.

As part of their time in the camp, enrollees learned how to plan a workday, make a good roadbed, and cut and lay sandstone. The camp's organized safety program included a committee that held weekly meetings and put up safety posters. As enrollees were discharged, national and state employment offices assisted them in finding work. The vocational training received at the camps turned out a varied group of trained workers.

Construction on the new visitor center building began in 1935. The building is still in use today. George Miller used his adze to shape the timbers that are visible in the main lobby area. Normally, these timbers came rough and the texture changed as he worked and shaped them—that was one way he gauged his progress. But when the timbers for the administration building arrived they were planed and sanded Douglas Fir. Miller's solution was to coat the surface of the timbers with blue carpenter's chalk. Then, he was able to gauge his progress.

Howard W. Baker was the resident landscape architect who chose northern Spanish architecture for the building styles. He felt it blended in with the area as it was somewhat rustic. As the work progressed, a sense of pride grew right along with the buildings. The men were learning marketable skills and trades for future employment, making money, and helping their families. Living conditions and work efforts contributed to good camp morale. Enrollees had opportunities to take classes in many subjects, from bookkeeping and blueprinting to cooking and journalism. A weekly camp newspaper, called *The Windjammer,* was produced, giving more on-the-job training for aspiring journalists.

The new visitor center building was completed by the CCC, but something was missing.

It was the landscaping.

There were very few trees on the headquarters property when the CCC first came to the park. The pine trees were dug up very carefully with picks and shovels, moved and transplanted around the visitor center.

As the trees were dug out of the ground, they were wrapped in burlap to hold the dirt in place around the roots.

The tree ball was loaded onto a truck to move it to the desired location. Over 1,200 trees were transplanted with such care that not one of them died, as the story goes.

This group of men included park and CCC personnel as well as civilian contractors. Next to the 1934 Chevrolet, from left to right, areas follows: Tom Sawyer; Lieutenant Henry; Estes Suter; two unidentified men; Floyd Dawkins, who worked in the Game Preserve, in the white shirt and tie; bow-tied man, unknown; Dixon Freeland; and Bill Englebert. Bill was a plumber from Hot Springs who was hired on for the plumbing work as needed. Paul Broyles, one of Edward Freeland's grandsons, was employed at the cave in the early 1980s.

Lieutenant Henry was the Army Reserve officer who was in charge of the Civilian Conservation Corps at Wind Cave. The dog is not named, but the pet coon in the lieutenant's hands is Tony.

The woman with her hand on the car was Mrs. Tom (Hazel) Sawyer. The other two are not known. They are standing in front of the Wind Cave Lunch Room with the errand vehicle.

The errand vehicle was used mostly by Estes Suter to gather supplies from Hot Springs, transport the children living at Wind Cave—including his own and Dale Sawyer—to school. Estes went to town every day and ran errands for everyone. He picked up laundry, bought greeting cards—whatever people needed him to do. Tom Sawyer is in the photo in front of the lunch room and Estes Suter took the photo.

Sandstone walls were built, or in this case moved, to allow the road to be widened in the area of the visitor center and the residences. Wheelbarrows, stonecutting tools, cement mixers, and hand tools were in continuous use.

Stone guardrails in the headquarters area prevented accidents and unified the appearance of the access road.

The completed rock wall or guardrail served a decorative yet functional purpose. Samuel Anderson, originally from Chancellor, South Dakota, worked on these stone walls. He was with the CCC for three years in one capacity or another. He must have been a fast learner, because within three months of his enrollment, he was made a section leader.

One of Ray Millard's donated photos shows the back side of the new visitor center. The walk way to the elevator shaft had not been completed and the stone work along the road had not been finished yet when the photo was taken in 1935. The smaller building on hill was the dormitory for some of the rangers.

Tom Sawyer was standing in the doorway of the stucco-finished power plant, or light plant. The engine can be seen in the background.

The first electrical system was installed in 1931. When the CCC rewired the cave, beginning in 1938, the workers transported the wire cables in the same manner as it was done in this 1931 photo.

The electrical cables were awkward, heavy, and long, but with a team of men, the job was soon accomplished. The supervisor kept them all together. They passed in front of the visitor center and the concession building which was adjoining.

The long line of cable transporters finally reached the cave entrance and continued into the cave as far as was necessary. This process was repeated several times before the cables were all in place.

As visitation into the cave increased, improvements were needed to make a safer trail. Every piece of wood needed to build the forms for new concrete steps had to be carried in. These steps were near the area in the cave called the Fairgrounds. One man known to have worked on the steps was Melvin Kilian, originally from Gettysburg, South Dakota.

A rather ingenious system was created to move the concrete from the cement mixer, down a chute, and into the cave. Volney Bahr is at the top of the chute and Elsward Stutzman is loading the wheelbarrow in this 1935 photo.

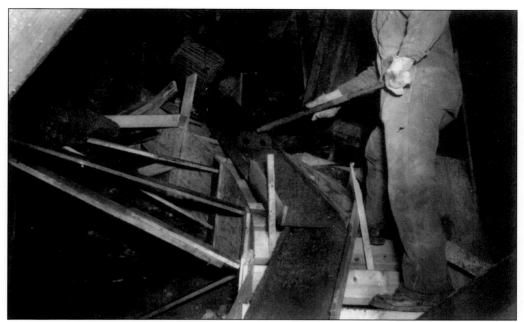

A wooden chute was built to guide the concrete on its way into the cave. The photo shows the view looking up the first flight of stairs toward the cave entrance.

Once the concrete was down the chute, some of it had to be transported inside inner tubes to get it where it needed to go. The tubes kept the concrete from splattering and dripping and could be carried around the neck. Wheelbarrows were used when it was possible but many places were not so accessible. William Hanson is wielding the shovel and filling the inner tube held by Elsward Stutzman. Volney Bahr has a loaded tube on his shoulders, ready to move the concrete to its destination. They were working in the area named Fallen Flats.

The man in this photo is unidentified. Henry Burg, of rural Hot Springs, told how he helped prepare for this stair work in 1933, with the Works Progress Administration (WPA), which was another federal work program at the time. Burg said, "George Anderson, Vigil Ashmore, Wilbur Cole, Snyder, and I were WPA. I drove 25 miles each way and was late to work only once in three months. That was when we had three feet of snow, and I had to hitch the team to the car in order to get it to the highway. Of course I had to unhitch the horses and feed them before I could go on to work. In the cave, Cole, Ashmore, and I crawled to the spot where we were to drill as there was no walkway yet. We had drills that we hit with a 12- or 14-pound sledge hammer. At night other workers dynamited where we drilled. The next day we would go in and use shovels to take out what we couldn't get with our hands. We would throw the debris into the crevices and side passageways. Then drill again. We were trying to make room for the steps that were planned. We were glad to have the work and made enough money to put food on the table, probably about 35¢ an hour. We worked until March when the CCC came in, then I went back to my farm to put in my crops." This interview is in the Wind Cave written archives.

The forms were filled with concrete. After the concrete was adequately dry, the forms were stripped off and the wooden forms were carried out of the cave, piece by piece just like they came in. Once the forms were removed in this area called the Bachelors Quarters, Byram Waller walked up the steps before railings were installed in 1936.

The wooden steps and hand rails had all been replaced by concrete steps and steel hand rails. The wooden stairs had been steeper and more slippery, and the wooden handrails tended to put wood slivers into the hands that used them. These stairs are located near the natural entrance.

Ranger Fred Lee led a tour down the concrete steps in this 1936 tour through the Fairgrounds room.

Rails were installed as needed to keep people on the trails provided.

A winding stairway was necessary due to the formations and characteristics within the cave.

# *Four*
# MEMORIES AND PEOPLE

As visitation increased, so did the number of vehicles in the parking lot at the visitor center. The first car is a Model A Ford from 1930 or 1931, and the third car in the line is a 1936 Buick or Pontiac.

In August of 1931 the Wind Cave rangers included, from left to right, as follows: (kneeling) Superintendent Freeland, Hackett, unknown, McKinney, Estes Suter, and Hart; (second row) Toflefson, unknown, Ted Perrin, Frogue, Tom Sawyer, Chambers, unknown, Lessard, Upton, unknown, and Wilcox.

There were only a few changes in the ranger staff by the time this August 1932 photo was taken. Pictured from left to right are as follows: (front row) Superintendent Edward Dixon Freeland; Glenn McKinney, lawyer; Arthur Rowden, music student; Charley Frogue, chemistry teacher; and Dick Wilcox, medical student; (second row) Hugh Miller, office clerk; Ellis Hacket, university student; John Chambers, the oldest guide; Howard Stricklin, drama teacher; Lanning Lessard, master of radio; and Estes Sutre, permanent ranger; (third row) Ted Perrin, medical student; Bob Upton, school teacher; Ronnie Robertson, student at School of Mines; Thomas Sawyer, eligible ranger; Ellery Kelly, professor in Hot Springs; Oscar Toflefson, professor in Gettysburg, South Dakota; and Wilbur Swanson, college student.

The rangers were nearly unrecognizable when they wore civilian clothing.

Pictured in this 1938 photo, from left to right, are Estes Suter, Howard Sticklin, Edward Freeland, John Chambers, and Perkins. Jodpurs were the style of uniform pants worn at the time.

The Hot Springs 8th grade class is seen here visiting Wind Cave on October 31, 1938, for a Halloween party. Pictured from left to right are as follows: (front row) McCloud, Bob Eiler, Ted Hagen, Raymond Rossknecht, Kenneth Kasitz, Maurice Asemusson, Bill Wilcox, Jack Hopper, Clifford Welch, Vern Bersch, James Blaisdel, Bob Parkinson, and Paul Davis; (second row) Ray Solberg, Ludwig Krein, Linton Schaffer, Kenneth Kasner, Donald Mueller, Charles Conger, Bob Neifer, Hollis O'Brien, Bob Hansen, Beverly Welick, Barbara Trumball, Jean Roberts, Betty Beswick, Bonnie Colburn, and Jack Humphrey; (third row) Foster Taylor, John Weisz, Harvey Helmer, Vesta Nelson, Gloria Jelle, Olga Kindopp, Effie Taylor, Barbara Crockford, Mildred Menuey, and June Vorce; (fourth row) teacher, Louise Weyl, Dorothy DeWitt, Shirley March, Barbara Conger, Luella ?, Loretta Thomas, Dorothy Shann, Esther Kaiser, Genevive Gallagher, and Roberta Husted; (fifth row) Alrene McCullough, Florence McFarland, Marjorie White, Phyllis Freeland, Dorothy Wilson, unknown, Rose Enid Nicklin, Shirley Wilcox, Velma Ream, Peggy Butler, Mary Brady, Helen Hibbard, LuAnn Shaul, unknown, Dorothy Dyke, Lester Thomas, Don Getty, and Arthur Jansen; (back row) unknown, Jerry Kelly, three unknown, Harry Knisley, Donna McDowell, Iva Collins, ? Finley, Charles Hemler, and Gale Watson, junior high principal and guide. Watson served as a guide at Wind Cave and also at Jewel Cave for many summers. The photo and caption were supplied by Dorothy DeWitt Craft.

The CCC and this 1934 Chevy truck were put to work on all sorts of jobs.

Buffalo fencing was put in by the CCC. Notice the height of the fence posts, the uneven terrain, and the snowy conditions.

In 1939, the jodhpur look, at least in the way of uniforms, had passed by the wayside.

New uniforms were introduced by 1941. Identified rangers in this photo are: front left, Glen Frary and third from left, Estes Suter. In the back row is Superintendent Harry Like. The others are not identified.

# *Five*

# INDIAN SUMMER ENCAMPMENT

For several summers a group of Lakota Sioux traveled from the Pine Ridge Indian Reservation to follow the rodeo circuit in the Black Hills. They had powwows and additional social events at places like Gold Discovery Days in Custer, The Days of '76 in Deadwood, and the Black Hills Roundup at Belle Fourche. The present day Butler Park in Hot Springs was then called the Pow Wow Grounds, as that was where they held one of their events for tourists. They traveled caravan style and Wind Cave National Park was one of their stopovers.

Chief Dan Blue Horse was the leader of the small group. He did not speak English, so he had to speak through the interpreter, Charlie Eagle Louse, as he answered questions as to how things used to be done.

When the Indians camped on Beaver Creek, east of Peter's Puddle and the Game Ranch, the park always gave them a buffalo to eat. Estes Suter cultivated relationships with the Indians when they came to the park on their annual pilgrimage to the Black Hills; he was the one who went out to the herd and shot the animal.

After the buffalo was dead, ropes were used to winch the heavy animal into the pickup so it could be transported to the encampment.

As the butchering was in progress, care was taken to not destroy the paunch, or rumen (on which the man's hand rests). The hide was laid out so the butchering could take place on it. Every part of the buffalo but the "beller" was used either by the Indians or by the park staff.

The ribs and rib meat were removed in one fell swoop to yield a rack of ribs from the buffalo.

After the paunch was emptied, it became this cooking vessel mounted on stakes. Hot rocks were put in, water was added so it would boil, and then the food. This was the same way it used to be done out on the trail.

In Indian tradition, the elders were served first and the oldest man, 90-year-old White Cow Bull, got the delicacies from the buffalo bull. White Cow Bull knew General Custer and fought at the Battle of Little Big Horn.

The three elders are, from left to right, White Cow Bull, Laughing Bear, and White Wolf. With the help of Eagle Louse, Suter was able to find out from White Cow Bull which buffalo bull in the herd was the most perfect specimen on which to base the park's buffalo breeding program. Since White Cow Bull had seen buffalo roaming about on the prairie, he knew what characteristics were desirable for bloodlines in a herd. Suter wanted to build a herd that was as close to perfect as possible— and who better to tell him than an Indian elder who had been there.

The camps were set up in an open area in the park. Generally the group arrived in mid-July, remained in this camp for about a week, and then the time was right for them to move on to Custer and Gold Discovery Days.

Mrs. White Wolf was right in the thick of things when the buffalo was butchered and cooked.

These elders were having a great time, eating raw liver from the buffalo—another treat for them. The youngsters were not as eager to eat it, though some of them tried. They had developed other tastes, for such things as ice cream.

Vera Blue Horse seems to be intently watching something on the ground. The Suter children enjoyed it when the Indians camped, as there was much to learn and new kids with whom to play.

When the buffalo was cut up, the meat was divided, with portions for each family unit, and piled on the interior of the freshly skinned hide. Each family could then pick up their portions.

Mrs. White Wolf was holding up the edges of the buffalo hide, perhaps signaling people to come for their meat supplies.

The women prepared parts of the meal in front of their tents. The long dresses were their everyday apparel.

Vera Blue Horse is carrying a toddler who doesn't look very happy.

Part of the buffalo meat was hung to dry and became jerky. Once it was dried it was preserved and traveled well. It is puzzling as to why this meat did not attract flies.

After the family groups picked up their meat, the hide was stretched and held down by stakes so it would dry flat.

The four men standing in a group were drumming and singing as they did for powwows.

Several of the Indians donned their ceremonial clothes and posed for this group photo. In the center is Superintendent Freeland, sporting a headdress that the Indians gave him to wear.

Many of the men traveled on horseback, with a bedroll behind the saddle and a rifle in the scabbard.

The main park highway used to run in front of the visitor center and the caravan came along the same route. The Lakota words for Wind Cave are *Washun Niya*, which means breathing hole.

*Six*

# THE LAST 50 YEARS

The year 1953 was a milestone as Wind Cave celebrated 50 years under the umbrella of the National Park Service. Park ranger Estes Suter posed for this photo with two friends of his son John. John and his friends were all employed as firefighters for the California Department of Forestry. John brought the others, who were both from Athens, Tennessee, to visit the park.

**"WHERE THE BUFFALO ROAM..."**

The scene before you is typical of the extensive buffalo country of pioneer days. Rolling grasslands, sheltering groves, and scattered waterholes of Wind Cave National Park support about 300 bison today. _Watch for them_

About 5,000 remain in this country, which once supported millions.

Large bison may weigh a ton

calf                    cow                    bull                    Some reach 40 years in age

American "buffalo" are correctly called *bison*, since true buffaloes are found only in the Old World

They feed on grass and herbs

This sign was in the park for many years. It detailed information on the buffalo. Signage change occurs as the park evolves.

The park tries to keep their herd at about 400 head. When they have excess buffalo, they are generally given to Indian tribes to be used as they wish, whether for breeding stock or to butcher.

Bison are rounded up nearly every year for herd health reasons such as vaccinations.. Each one is weighed and their ages are recorded. With the new technology, computer chips are inserted for record keeping. Old or infirm animals are culled.

This is an example of why you do not approach buffalo. They are wild animals and they will come after you. In this instance, two bulls were fighting during mating season near several cars that were lined up on the highway, the occupants watching the bulls. The losing bull took the lowest route available—the shortest car in this case—to escape. The owner of the Karmen Ghia had the park service write a letter to his insurance company to explain what caused the damage.

Before the improved highway was completed in 1967, with a bypass around the park headquarters, hundreds of trucks had passed by the administration building. This particular one appears to be making a delivery to the park.

After he returned from his service in the Korean War, V. Francis Varick was hired as a mechanic for the park.

This photo was taken on Snow Drift Avenue, north of the Pearly Gates, in the cave. The men were Don Frankfort, on the top left, and Rich Lawther. A camera flash provided the light.

The Fairgrounds was discovered and recorded in 1892. The largest room open to the public, it is part of the longest tour offered within the cave which takes one and a half hours to complete. The other tours are the Natural Entrance Tour with a time frame of one hour and 15 minutes, and the Garden of Eden Tour, which takes one hour. The paths for all tours are hard-surfaced for ease in walking.

After the buffalo are rounded up each year, they are "worked" by park personnel and local veterinarians. The alley way on the edge of this corral guides the buffalo into the chute area. At this point, the men stay on the catwalk, which brings them up above the buffalo and keeps them out of the small, enclosed pens.

As the buffalo that need vaccinations for preventative measures walk into the chute, the workers close gates and catch the head of the buffalo. After years of selective breeding, a program started by Estes Suter, the Wind Cave herd is considered to be exemplary.

Once the animal is secure in the head
catch, vaccinations and any other
medical needs can be attended to.

One of these men is Stan Stenson, an employee
of Custer State Park in 1960; the other man
is not identified. A syringe is being filled with
medication that will be injected into a buffalo.

A phone in the elevator is used for official calls. Looking back, before the Rural Electric Administration (REA) was in existence bringing electricity to the park and the areas beyond, the phone was a must. At that time, if someone wanted to use the elevator, he had to call ahead to the powerhouse so all of the power emitted from the four-cylinder diesel motor could be utilized by the elevator.

Park Ranger Lee and visitors are pictured here as they complete the cave tour and return to the surface. The pants worn by the woman were called pedal pushers. They are in style again in 2003 but are called capris.

The cave electrical system shows a modern junction point for 2,400 volt distribution at essential points in the cave. Number 1 is a compound sealed pot head. Arrow 2 shows the metal gates that were installed to prevent visitors' access to dangerous voltages.

Conduit encases the electric lines throughout the cave. This is a typical low voltage relay and circuit breaker station. Illustrated in number one are relay boxes that are operated by a 24-volt mercury-type switch. Number 2 details the Westinghouse circuit breakers used throughout the project to protect the 240-volt circuit.

Rankin Ridge was named after the first superintendent of the park, William A. Rankin, who began his job on August 1, 1903. It is located on the north end of the park and is the highest point in the park at 5,013 feet.

A steel fire tower was under construction on Rankin Ridge. It replaced the wooden one that had been built there in 1952.

Pictured here is the completed fire lookout tower on Rankin Ridge. The room at the top housed one person. At least 25 of these observation posts were located in the Black Hills when Clara Marvin worked the tower called Flag Mountain near Deerfield, South Dakota. Clara's daughter, now Phyllis Schiefer of Hot Springs, started on Flag Mountain as the alternate for her mom. Since Flag Mountain, Phyllis has manned Battle Mountain, Rankin Ridge, and Bear Mountain towers. She still works a tower if called, although most area towers are not staffed any more.

Watching areas like this for fires, especially after lightening storms, kept the lookout busy. Periodically the park does prescribed burns to clear unwanted undergrowth, following the belief that fires can be part of a forest management system.

Lynn Frary is shown working in the fire tower. The maps were used to direct firefighters to locations once smoke was seen. The best combination was if at least one other tower could also see the smoke. Each tower would give their Azimuth circle coordinates, shown on the map, to other towers that could see the fire. Strings were placed on the map to see where the coordinates crossed, which showed the fire's location. The better each worker knew his area, the more exactly he could direct the fire crews.

Living quarters were part of the tower facilities. A water tank on the roof of the tower provided a gravity-fed water supply. A propane refrigerator and stove, plus a bed were the accommodations. The water tank was filled by a "pumper truck." There was no electricity, only a glass lantern for light. An outhouse, or "porta-potty," was located on the ground, down the 74 steps. When it was staffed, visitors were welcome. A typical shift was five days on and two days off with an alternate working the days off. Because workers were considered part of the fire crew, the replacements were other fire crew members. If a fire started up, even when it was during the days off, the regular tower worker would go back to work freeing the alternate to fight the fire.

Binoculars were used to spot fires. Spotting scopes came into use later. Battery powered two-way radios were the main source of contact with authorities. For many years, if lightning was in the area, the radio antenna had to be disconnected during the storm and no reports could be made until the lightening had passed. That problem has been resolved.

Lightning is not the only cause of forest fires. On hot, dry days, sparks from a piece of equipment or a vehicle can start fires. When lightning does strike, it is often the next day before the fire will show up. Even if other parts of the tree are on fire, and rain puts it out, the root will still smolder for hours before it emits smoke and can be spotted. Fire observers were employed to keep scenes like this large fire from happening often. Rankin Ridge tower, like many in the Black Hills, is no longer staffed. It is used only on occasion and is not open to the public.

"AND THE ANTELOPE PLAY..."

The fleet pronghorn antelope has been clocked at 60 miles per hour. This speed and remarkably sharp vision help the pronghorn survive in open country. Thousands still flourish on the Great Plains. About 130 live in Wind Cave National Park. They often graze within view of park roads.

heavy ones weigh 135 pounds

The "prong" on the horn is the source of the name

Only pronghorn antelope shed their horns yearly, unlike the permanent horns of bison, cattle and true antelopes of the Old World

buck          doe          kid

They eat grass and shrubs                     some reach 7 years in age

Called antelope, these animals are actually pronghorn. They can run as fast as 60 miles per hour, with sustained speeds of 30 miles per hour. They can easily jump a 4-foot high fence and can jump much further horizontally than vertically.

Here we see the joys of motherhood for this pronghorn doe and her fawn, inhabitants of the park. Pronghorn or antelope are generally seen in fairly large herds as they adhere to the "safety in numbers" concept, which helps protect them from predators.

In the foreground is a cattle guard, a series of pipes welded together into one unit and placed over a shallow pit that had been dug to accommodate the guard. Bison, cattle, horses, and other large animals will not generally cross a cattle guard, so they can be installed at road points along a fence line. This allows people in vehicles to cross the fence lines without having to get out and open gates.

There is a lot more to managing the park than watching the buffalo roam and the antelope play. This moisture study grid from August 23, 1956 shows a range plot study.

This staff photo taken during the summer of 1980 shows, from left to right, as follows: (front row) Bill Holmes, Don Frankfort, Phil Dodge, Gordon Messling, Brenda Messling, and Chuck Bertsch; (second row) Tina Yee, Norm Salisbury, Sue Burden, Mary Laycock, Kim Mogen, Bob Hirschy, and Jeri Kizer; (back row) Dan Culliname, Barb Brutvan, Terese Hackenberg, Gail Pickut, Lynn Hetlet, Larry Frederick, Tom Farrell, and Woody Pickut.

In the summer of 1981 these staff members dressed in period costume and presented a living history candlelight tour of the cave. This photo was taken in the Silent Lake Room. Pictured from left to right in the front row are Kim Mogen, Barb Brutvan, Gordon Messling, and Mary Laycock. Bob Hirschy, left, and Lynn Hetlet, right, held the 45 star flag which was flown beginning in 1896, after Utah became a state.

This group of cavers was celebrating the mapping of Wind Cave's 50th mile on August 15, 1987. John Scheltens is on the left; Ed LaRock is holding the book; and Jim Nepstad is the man in the center, and Al Williams is at the top. At the time of this publication, 106.8 surveyed miles have been recorded within the confines of Wind Cave.

Cavers on an exploration trip are shown here. A tour called the Wild Cave Tour is offered for the more adventurous cave visitors. Knee pads and hard hats with lights attached are some of the equipment necessary; they are furnished by the park.

In recent years it was determined that the asphalt used for the trails within the cave was detrimental and it had to be removed. The project began in 1986. An ax was used to break up the asphalt.

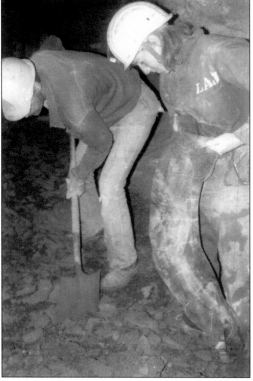

Inner tubes—again! Not much changed over all the years; everything still has to be packed in or packed out. Asphalt was shoveled into the inner tubes and hauled out. Some pathways were lowered so people did not need to stoop as they walked through the cave.

During the light removal and restoration project in 1988, old wires and metal conduit were removed. The hand tools in the foreground were used to do the work.

This cave restoration crew and the pile of junk removed from the cave were photographed outside the elevator building.

This pile of debris was removed during the 1988 lighting project when incandescent lights replaced the fluorescents.

This shows the reconstruction of the cave entrance and steps. The workers were at the bottom of the first flight of stairs near the entrance. They were setting blocks and using a hydraulic jack to test the footing support strength.

Out with the old asphalt, in with the new concrete—it was used to make new paths. Don Lytle, crew leader, was holding the inner tube and getting ready to make a drop. The other person is not named, but is identified as a National Outdoor Leadership School (NOLS) student.

Slow going—just a tube at a time—but the end result was worth it.

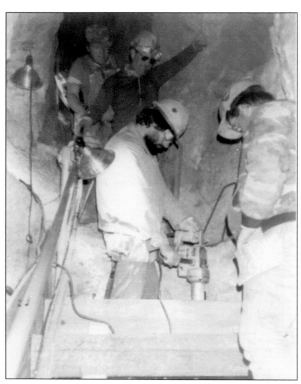

It was possible to use a jack hammer in places. The air compressor used to run the hammer sat outside the cave. The only man identified in this photo is Joe Allen, at back.

A chisel, whisk broom, and a shovel are contrasted with the air-powered jack hammer during this 1986 step restoration project.

A caver wears a hardhat with an attached light, knee pads, elbow pads, and comfortable clothing. In addition to caving for fun and adventure, cavers also served a practical purpose, working inside the cave. Often they had to search side passages for wires that had been hidden from view and were no longer in use.

This part of the cave's electrical system shows a portion of the bank of six photoflood concentrator fixtures emitting 500 watts each. These lights made it possible for photographic work to be done in the Temple Room.

Always looking for ways to protect the cave environment, this revolving door was installed in 1992.

Jean Donnell retired from her secretarial position in 1994 after 35 years of federal service. She is pictured in this earlier photo with her co-workers, from left to right, as follows: (front row) Nat Lacy, Dick Hart, Earl (Tiny) Semingsen, Estes Suter, and Keith Miller; (back row) Walt Powell, Harold Chittum, Jean Donnell, Edna Allen, Wes Warner, Bill Hanson, Evelyn Suter, and Bob Merrill. Currently, in 2003, the park hires 43 people year-round (including those subject to furlough) and between 50 and 55 seasonal workers.

Estes Suter took this photo in the course of his workday. Because he was especially observant and took his job so seriously, he saw, and recorded, what others may not have ever seen. This bird's nest in the prairie grass is an example of his attention to detail. At least 55 species of birds have been spotted in the park within the last 7 years.

This little fawn, sleeping by the trees where his mother told him to stay, is another example of Estes Suter's work. He not only was in the right place at the right time, he had a camera at the ready and took advantage of the moment.

John McDill Jr. started working at Wind Cave in May of 1974. He was part of the Wind Cave family for nearly all of his 24-year park service career. He is always seen with a big smile on his face, even after fighting a fire, lying at peace and at rest.

*As the park staff members look toward the future, they continue to preserve what the park has to offer and to learn, study, and teach as each new day unfolds in the park.*